I Can Read GOD'S WORD!

Born Again!

and other stories (from) the New Testament

BARBOUR
PUBLISHING

PHIL A. SMOUSE

*In him was life,
and that life was the light of men.*

John 1:4 NIV

ISBN 1-59310-099-X

Published by Barbour Publishing, Inc., P.O. Box 719, Uhrichsville, Ohio 44683
www.barbourbooks.com

Our mission is to publish and distribute inspirational products offering exceptional value and biblical encouragement to the masses.

Member of the
Evangelical Christian
Publishers Association

Printed in China.
5 4 3

CONTENTS

A NOTE TO PARENTS. . .

I Can Read God's Word! is a simple idea with a simple goal: to put the Word of God on the lips of God's children.

I've drawn from the practical teachings of Jesus in the New Testament and the promises of God in the Old and "translated" them into an easy-to-read paraphrase that is absolutely faithful to the original text while staying as close as possible to the phonics-based reading curriculum your children are learning at home or in school.

Twenty-three long years went by before
I ever read a single page of the Bible for
myself. But if God answers prayer (and you
know He does), before *this* year is over you
will hear a familiar little voice say, "Mom,
Dad, listen. . .*I Can Read God's Word!*"

Enjoy!

Phil A. Smouse

YOU WILL FIND ME

Matthew 7:7-8

Jesus said, "Ask."

"And it will be given!"

"Seek."

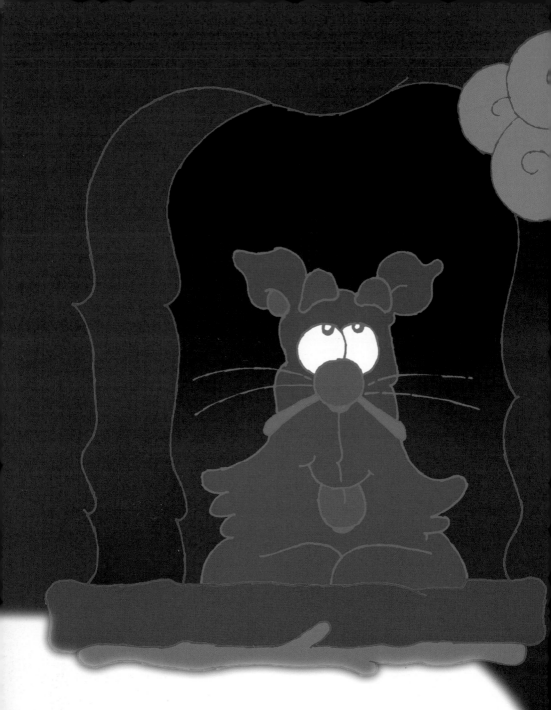

"And you will find!"

"Knock."

"And the door will open!"

"For everyone who asks
will get what he needs."

"Everyone who
looks for Me
will find Me."

"And when you knock,
I will open the door."

"I will welcome you inside!"

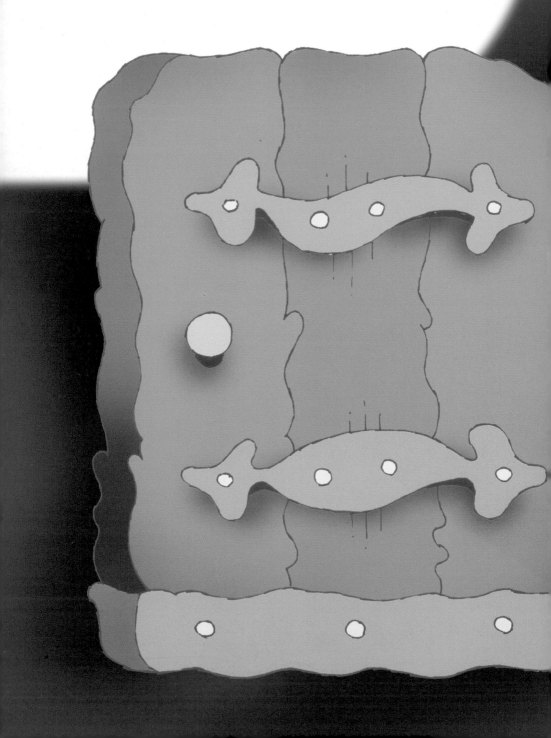

PEACE

Philippians 4:4-7

At all times,

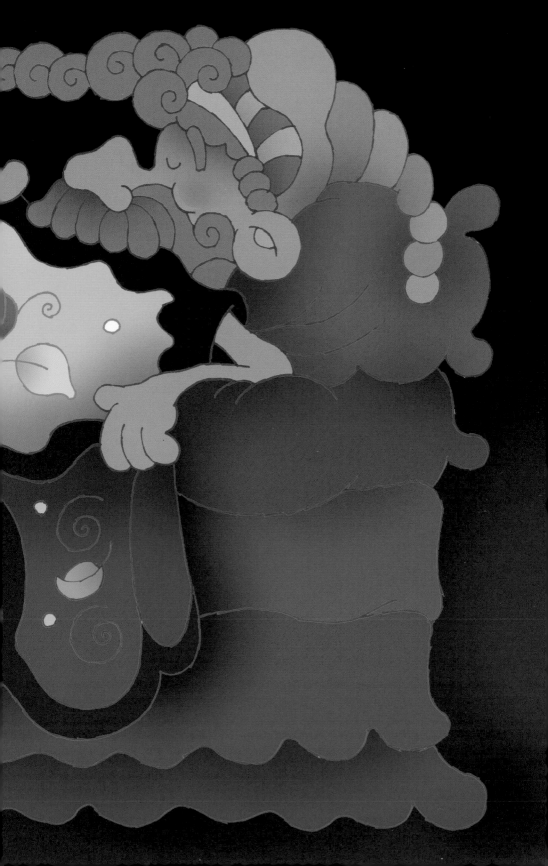

in every way,

in all things,

rejoice!

Let your heart
be filled with joy.

You do not need to worry.

God hears your prayers.

Tell God what you want.

Tell Him what you need.

Then give Him thanks!

And God's peace
will guard your heart.
God's peace will guard
your mind. You will
trust in Him!

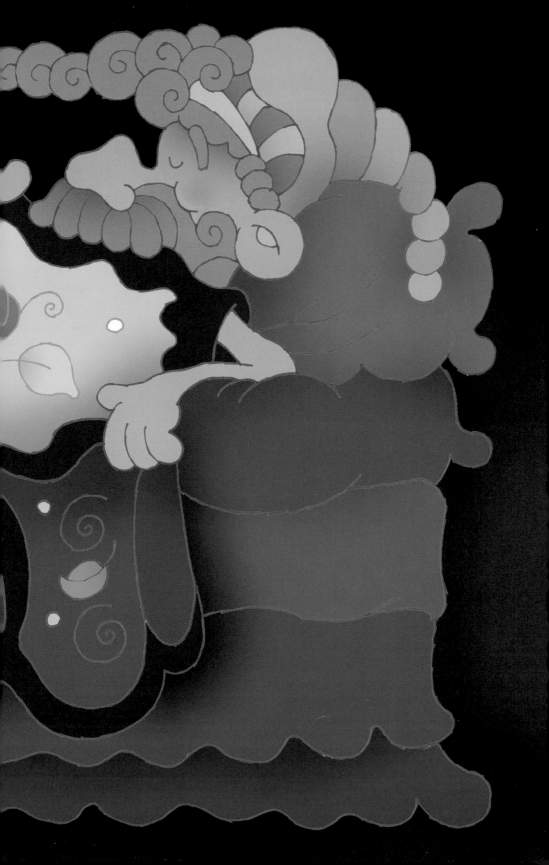

BORN AGAIN!

John 3:3-7, 16-17

Jesus said,
"You must be
born again!"

"But how?" a wise man asked.

"I will tell you!"
said Jesus.

"Long ago your mother
gave birth to your *body*.
You were born
for the first time."

"God wants to give you a *new* life on the *inside.* God wants His Spirit to live deep down inside your *heart.*"

So. . .

"You must be born *again*! You must be God's child."

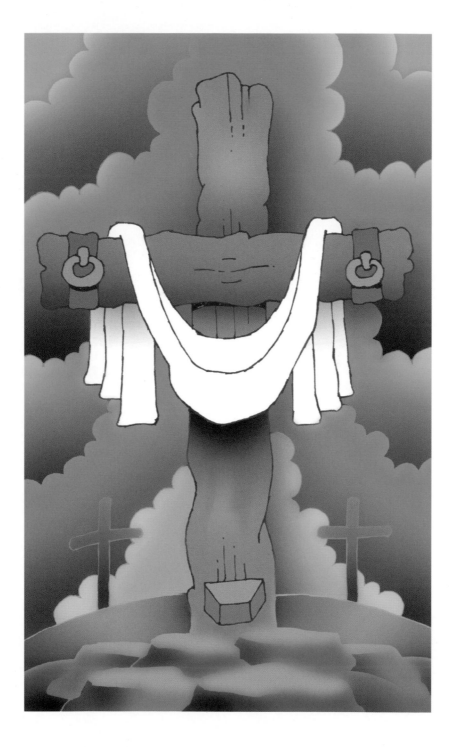

"Why are you surprised?"
Jesus asked the man.

"God loved the world
so much He gave His
only Son. All who believe
in God's Son will never
die. They will live with
God in heaven.
Forever!"

ALL THINGS ARE NEW

2 Corinthians 5:17

Jesus loves you.
Jesus died to set you
free from sin.

When this happens,
the "old you" is gone.
God forgives your sins.

You can start over right now.

God makes you
new inside.
All things are new!

YOU WILL FIND ME
Matthew 7:7–8

"Ask, and it will be given to you; seek, and you will find; knock, and it will be opened to you. For everyone who asks receives, and he who seeks finds, and to him who knocks it will be opened."

PEACE
Philippians 4:4–7

Rejoice in the Lord always. Again I will say, rejoice! Let your gentleness be known to all men. The Lord is at hand. Be anxious for nothing, but in everything by prayer and supplication, with thanksgiving, let your requests be made known to God; and the peace of God, which surpasses all understanding, will guard your hearts and minds through Christ Jesus.

BORN AGAIN!
John 3:3–7, 16–17

"Most assuredly I say to you, unless one is born again, he cannot see the kingdom of God." Nicodemus said to Him, "How can a man be born when he is old? Can he enter a second time into his mother's womb and be born?" Jesus answered, "Most assuredly I say to you, unless one is born of water and the Spirit, he cannot enter the kingdom of God. That which is born of the flesh is flesh, and that which is born of the Spirit is spirit. Do not marvel that I said to you, 'You must be born again.'

"For God so loved the world that He gave His only begotten Son, that whoever believes in Him should not perish but have everlasting life. For God did not send His Son into the world to condemn the world, but that the world through Him might be saved."

ALL THINGS ARE NEW
2 Corinthians 5:17

Therefore, if anyone is in Christ, he is a new creation; old things have passed away; behold, all things have become new.